THE SUPER SONGBOOK FOR KIDS

Order No. AM983532
ISBN 978.0.8256.3464.2

Designed & art directed by Michael Bell Design.
Illustrated by Sonia Canals.

Exclusive distributors:
Music Sales Corporation
257 Park Avenue South, New York, NY 10010, USA.
Music Sales Limited
14-15 Berners Street, London, W1T 3LJ, England.
Music Sales Pty. Limited
120 Rothschild Street, Rosebery, Sydney, NSW 2018, Australia.

Printed in Peru by Quebecor World

AMSCO PUBLICATIONS
part of The Music Sales Group

London / New York / Paris / Sydney / Copenhagen / Berlin / Madrid / Tokyo

ALICE THE CAMEL

Traditional

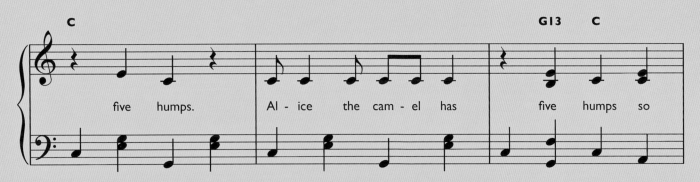

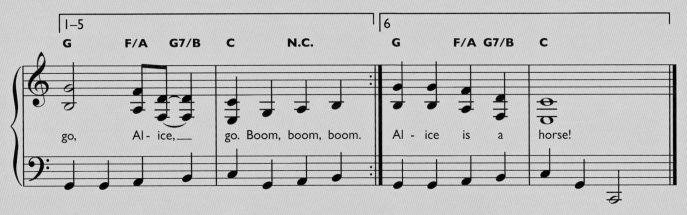

2

Alice the camel has four humps.
Alice the camel has four humps.
Alice the camel has four humps
So go, Alice, go.
Boom, boom, boom.

3

Alice the camel has three humps.
Alice the camel has three humps.
Alice the camel has three humps
So go, Alice, go.
Boom, boom, boom.

4

Alice the camel has two humps.
Alice the camel has two humps.
Alice the camel has two humps
So go, Alice, go.
Boom, boom, boom.

5

Alice the camel has one hump.
Alice the camel has one hump.
Alice the camel has one hump
So go, Alice, go.
Boom, boom, boom.

6

Alice the camel has no humps.
Alice the camel has no humps.
Alice the camel has no humps
So Alice is a horse!

THE SUPER SONGBOOK FOR KIDS

ANIMAL FAIR

Traditional

Brightly, in two (♩. = one beat)

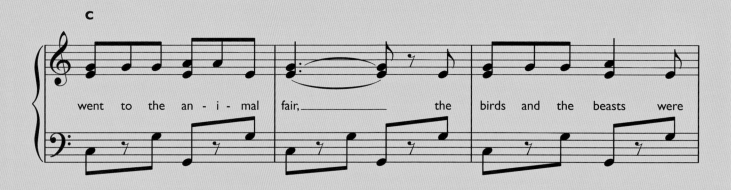

went to the an - i - mal fair,_____ the birds and the beasts were

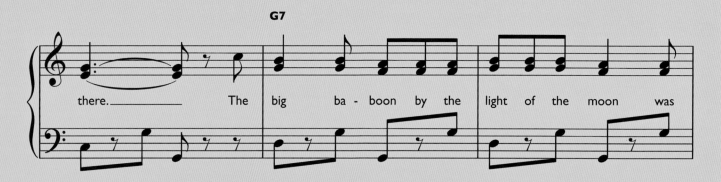

there._____ The big ba - boon by the light of the moon was

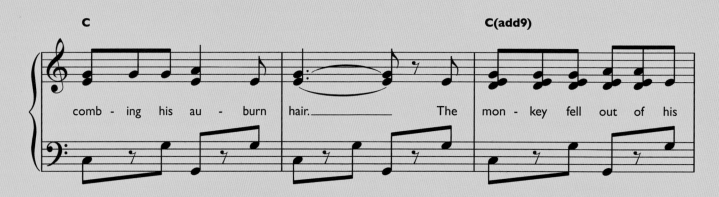

comb - ing his au - burn hair._____ The mon - key fell out of his

BINGO

Traditional

With a bounce

1.There was a farm-er had a dog, and Bin-go was his name-o.

*B - I - N-G-O! B - I - N-G-O!

B - I - N-G-O! And Bin-go was his name - o!

As you sing through
verses 2-6,
replace each letter with
a clap, as shown.

2
There was a farmer had a dog,
And Bingo was his name-o.
(clap)-I-N-G-O!
(clap)-I-N-G-O!
(clap)-I-N-G-O!
And Bingo was his name-o!

3
There was a farmer had a dog,
And Bingo was his name-o.
(clap, clap)-N-G-O!
(clap, clap)-N-G-O!
(clap, clap)-N-G-O!
And Bingo was his name-o!

4
There was a farmer had a dog,
And Bingo was his name-o.
(clap, clap, clap)-G-O!
(clap, clap, clap)-G-O!
(clap, clap, clap)-G-O!
And Bingo was his name-o!

5
There was a farmer had a dog,
And Bingo was his name-o.
(clap, clap, clap, clap)-O!
(clap, clap, clap, clap)-O!
(clap, clap, clap, clap)-O!
And Bingo was his name-o!

6
There was a farmer had a dog,
And Bingo was his name-o.
(clap, clap, clap, clap, clap)
(clap, clap, clap, clap, clap)
(clap, clap, clap, clap, clap)
And Bingo was his name-o!

A FLY WALKED INTO A GROCERY STORE

Allegro

A fly walked in-to a gro — cery store, a-lone, tee-hee, all a-

FIVE LITTLE DUCKS

Traditional

Moderately

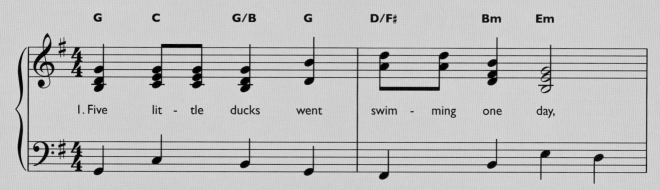

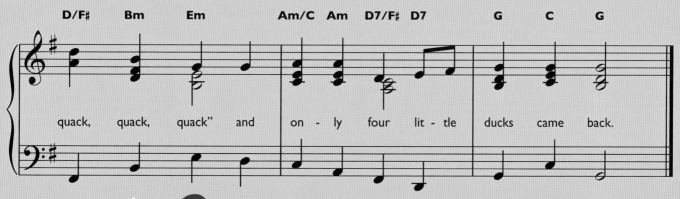

2 Four little ducks went swimming one day, *etc.*

3 Three little ducks went swimming one day, *etc.*

4 Two little ducks went swimming one day, *etc.*

5 One little duck went swimming one day,
Over the hills and far away.
The mother duck said, "Quack, quack, quack, quack"
And five little ducks came swimming right back.

Do Your Ears Hang Low?

Traditional

Lively (♪♪ = ³♩♪)

mf

1. Do your

ears hang low? Do they wob-ble to and fro? Can you tie 'em in a knot? Can you

2

Can your ears hang high?
Can they stand up to the sky?
Can they stand up if they're wet?
Can they stand up if they're dry?
Can you wave them to your neighbor with a minimum of labor?
Can your ears stand high?

Traditional

HERE WE GO LOOBY LOO

With movement

Here we go loo - by loo,   here we go loo - by light,

here we go loo - by loo, all on a Sat - ur - day night.

1. Put your right hand in, put your right hand out,

put your right hand in a - gain and shake it all____ a - bout.

2 Put your left hand in, *etc.*

3 Put your right arm in, *etc.*

Chorus
Here we go looby loo,
Here we go looby light,
Here we go looby loo,
All on a Saturday night.

4 Put your left arm in, *etc.*

5 Put your right foot in, *etc.*

6 Put your left foot in, *etc.*

7 Put your right leg in, *etc.*

8 Put your left leg in, *etc.*

9 Put your back in, *etc.*

10 Put your front in, *etc.*

11 Put your head in, *etc.*

12 Put your whole self in, *etc.*

FIVE LITTLE MONKEYS

Traditional

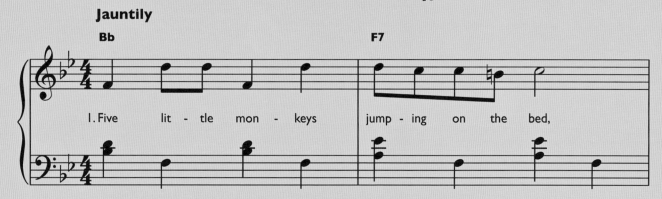

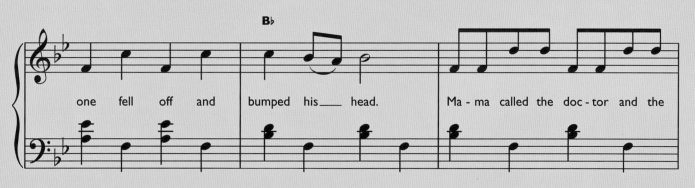

2 Four little monkeys, *etc.*

3 Three little monkeys, *etc.*

4 Two little monkeys, *etc.*

5 One little monkey, *etc.*

6 No more monkeys jumping on the bed.
No more monkeys bumping their head.
No more calling doctors, and doctors no more said,
"No more monkey business jumping on the bed!"

THE SUPER SONGBOOK FOR KIDS

IF ALL OF THE RAINDROPS

Traditional

Jolly

mf 1. If all of the rain - drops were lem - on drops and gum - drops,

2 If all of the snowflakes were candy bars and milkshakes,
Oh what a snow that would be!
I'd go outside with my mouth open wide.
Ah, ah, ah, ah, ah, ah, ah, ah, ah, ah.
If all of the snowflakes were candy bars and milkshakes,
Oh what a snow that would be!

GREASY GRIMY GOPHER GUTS

Traditional

Moderately

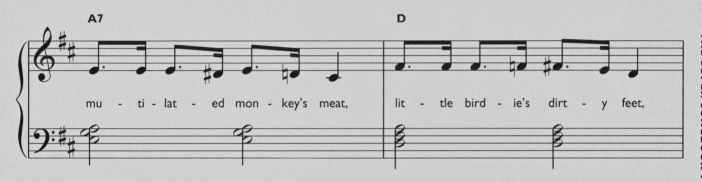

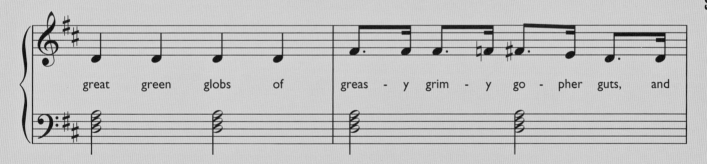

Great green globs of greas-y grim-y go-pher guts,
mu-ti-lat-ed mon-key's meat, lit-tle bird-ie's dirt-y feet,
great green globs of greas-y grim-y go-pher guts, and
I for-got my spoon!

THE SUPER SONGBOOK FOR KIDS

OLD MacDONALD HAD A FARM

Bright

Traditional

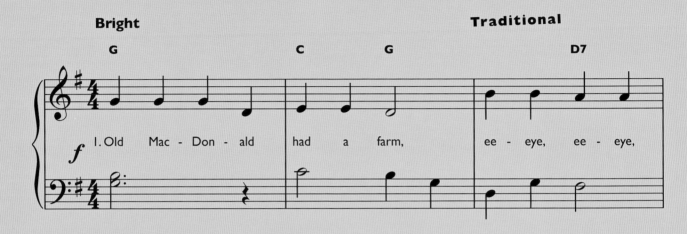

2 Old MacDonald had a farm,
Ee-eye, ee-eye, oh!
And on that farm he had some ducks,
Ee-eye, ee-eye, oh!
With a quack-quack here and a quack-quack there,
Here a quack, there a quack, everywhere a quack-quack.
Chick-chick here and a chick-chick there,
Here a chick, there a chick, everywhere a chick-chick.
Old MacDonald had a farm,
Ee-eye, ee-eye, oh!

3 ...and on that farm he had some cows...
With a moo-moo here and a moo-moo there,
Here a moo, there a moo, everywhere a moo-moo,
Quack-quack here and a quack-quack there...
Chick-chick here and a chick-chick there...

4 ...and on that farm he had some pigs...
With an oink-oink here and an oink-oink there,
Here an oink, there and oink, everywhere and oink-oink,
Moo-moo here...
Quack-quack here...
Chick-chick here...

5 ...and on that farm he had some sheep...
With a baa-baa here and a baa-baa there...

ACTIVITY

Repeat the song over and over, each time omitting a body part in the order that they are sung.

For example, the second time around you would point at your head but not actually say the word HEAD out loud.

The third time around you would leave out HEAD and SHOULDERS but still point to them.

Keep doing this until you are not actually saying anything – just pointing at the said body parts. You could also try getting faster and faster for an extra challenge!

HEAD, SHOULDERS, KNEES AND TOES

Fairly fast

Traditional

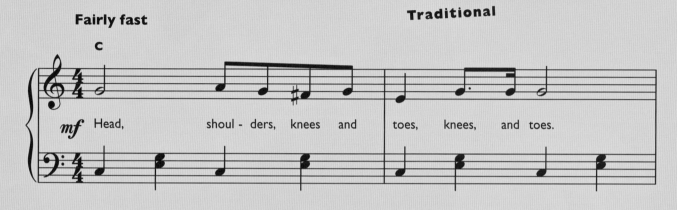

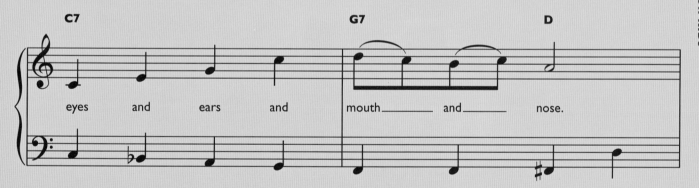

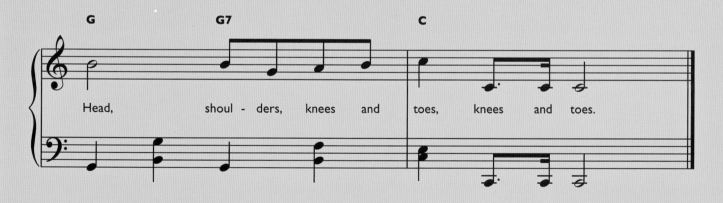

THE SUPER SONGBOOK FOR KIDS

IF YOU'RE HAPPY AND YOU KNOW IT

Traditional

2 ...stomp your feet, **(stomp, stomp)**, *etc.*

3 ...nod your head, **(nod, nod)**, *etc.*

4 ...turn around, **(turn around)**, *etc.*

5 ...touch your nose, **(touch nose)**, *etc.*

HERE WE GO 'ROUND THE MULBERRY BUSH

Traditional

With movement

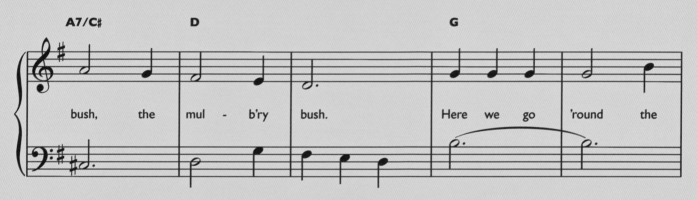

2 This is the way we go to school, *etc.*

3 This is the way we come back from school, *etc.*

4 This is the way we wash our hands, *etc.*

THE SUPER SONGBOOK FOR KIDS

I Know an Old Lady Who Swallowed a Fly

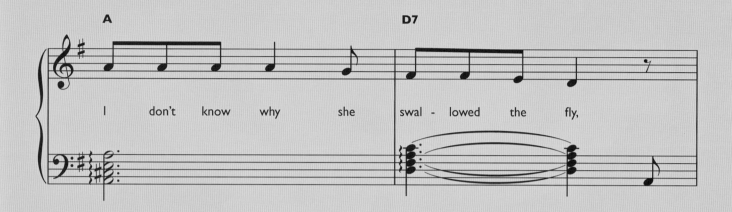

A | D7

I don't know why she swal - lowed the fly,

G | Fine | **D.S. al Fine**

per - haps she'll die! _____

3. 1

2 I know an old lady who swallowed a spider
That wriggled and jiggled and tickled inside her.
She swallowed the spider to catch the fly,
I don't know why she swallowed a fly,
Perhaps she'll die!

3 I know an old lady who swallowed a bird.
How absurd, to swallow a bird!
She swallowed the bird to catch the spider
That wriggled, *etc.*

4 I know an old lady who swallowed a cat,
Just fancy that, she swallowed a cat!
She swallowed the cat to catch the bird,
She swallowed the bird to catch the spider, *etc.*

5 I know an old lady who swallowed a dog,
What a hog, to swallow a dog!
She swallowed the dog to catch the cat,
She swallowed the cat to catch the bird, *etc.*

6 I know an old lady who swallowed a goat.
She just opened her throat and swallowed a goat!
She swallowed the goat to catch the dog,
She swallowed the dog to catch the cat, *etc.*

7 I know an old lady who swallowed a cow.
I don't know HOW she swallowed a cow.
She swallowed the cow to catch the goat,
She swallowed the goat to catch the dog, *etc.*

8 I know an old lady who swallowed a rhinoceros,
THAT'S PREPOSTEROUS!
She swallowed the rhino to catch the cow,
She swallowed the cow to catch the goat, *etc.*

9 I know an old lady who swallowed a horse.
She's dead, of course.

KUM BA YAH

With feeling

Traditional

1. Kum ba yah, my Lord, Kum ba yah! Kum ba yah, my Lord, Kum ba yah! Kum ba yah, my Lord, Kum ba yah! O Lord,___ Kum ba yah! 2. Some-one's yah! Hmm___

2 Someone's cryin', Lord, *etc.*   **3** Someone's singin', Lord, *etc.*   **4** Someone's shoutin', Lord, *etc.*

ITSY BITSY SPIDER

Moderately

Traditional

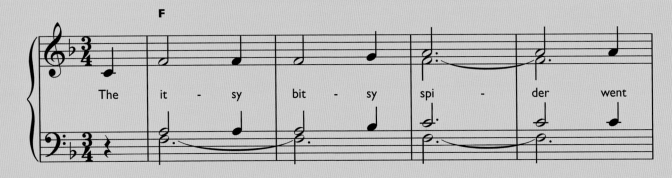

The it - sy bit - sy spi - der went

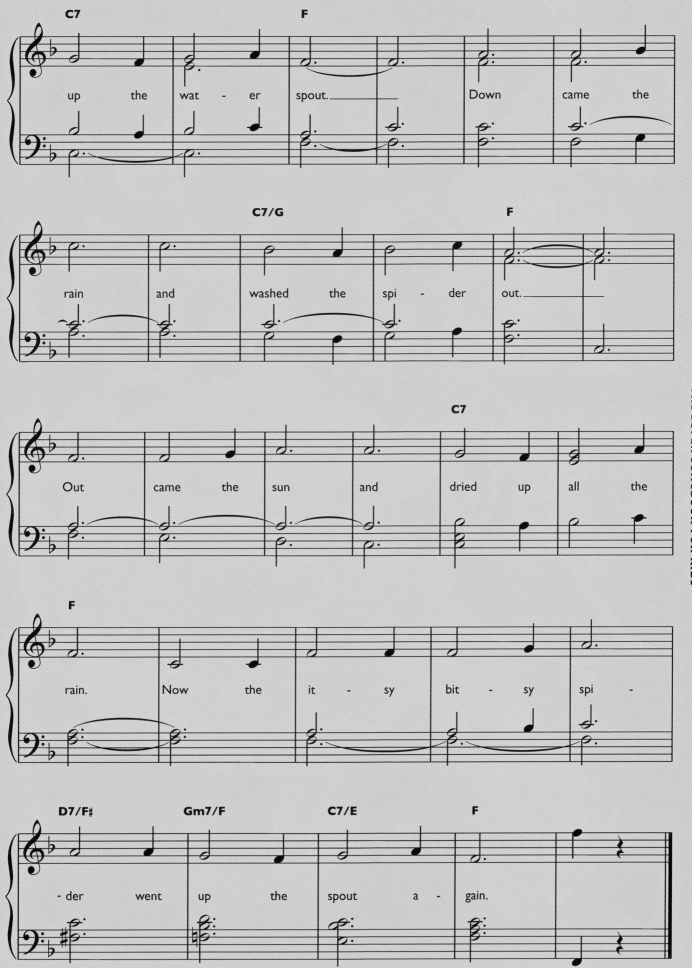

OH, WE CAN PLAY ON THE BIG BASS DRUM

Traditional

Moderately

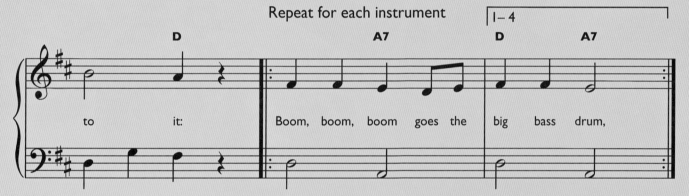

Repeat for each instrument

2 Oh, we can play on the tambourine,
And this is the music to it:
Chink, chink, chink goes the tambourine,
Boom, boom, boom goes the big bass drum,
And that's the way we do it.

3 Oh, we can play on the castanets,
And this is the music to it:
Click, clickety-click go the castanets,
Chink, chink, chink goes the tambourine,
Boom, boom, boom goes the big bass drum,
And that's the way we do it.

4 Oh, we can play on the triangle,
And this is the music to it:
Ping, ping, ping goes the triangle,
Click, clickety-click go the castanets,
Chink, chink, chink goes the tambourine,
Boom, boom, boom goes the big bass drum,
And that's the way we do it.

5 Oh, we can play on the old banjo,
And this is the music to it:
Tum, tum, tum goes the old banjo,
Ping, ping, ping goes the triangle,
Click, clickety-click go the castanets,
Chink, chink, chink goes the tambourine,
Boom, boom, boom goes the big bass drum,
And that's the way we do it.

THE SUPER SONGBOOK FOR KIDS

There Were Ten in the Bed

Traditional

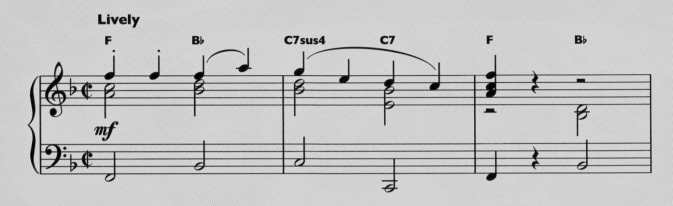

1.There were ten in the bed and the lit - tle one said, "Roll

o - ver, roll o - ver." So they all rolled o - ver and one fell out, he

bumped his head and gave a shout, "Ow! Please re - mem - ber to

tie a knot in your pa - ja - mas, sin - gle beds are on - ly meant for

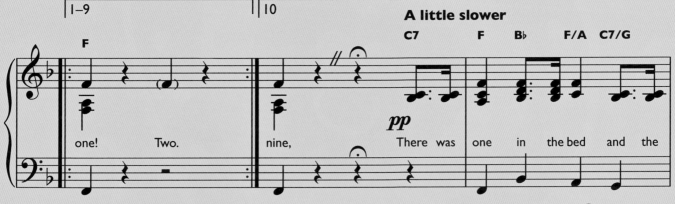

A little slower

one! Two. nine, *pp* There was one in the bed and the

lit – tle one said, "Good night,_____ good night!" _____

2 There were nine in the bed, *etc.*
...single beds are only made for
One, two!

3 There were eight in the bed, *etc.*
...single beds are only made for
One, two, three!

4 There were seven in the bed, *etc.*
...single beds are only made for
One, two, three, four!

5 There were six in the bed, *etc.*
...single beds are only made for
One, two, three, four, five!

6 There were five in the bed, *etc.*
...single beds are only made for
One, two, three, four, five, six!

7 There were four in the bed, *etc.*
...single beds are only made for
One, two, three, four, five, six, seven!

8 There were three in the bed, *etc.*
...single beds are only made for
One, two, three, four, five, six, seven, eight!

9 There were two in the bed, *etc.*
...single beds are only made for
One, two, three, four, five, six, seven, eight, nine!

10 There was one in the bed
And the little one said,
"Good night, good night!"

ON TOP OF OLD SMOKY

Traditional

Moderately

N.C.

F

mf 1.On top of Old Smok - y,_____ all

cov - ered with snow,_____ I

lost my true lov - - er,_____ by a-

- court - in' too slow._____

2 Well a-courting's a pleasure,
And parting is grief.
But a false-hearted lover
Is worse than a thief.

3 A thief he will rob you
And take all you have,
But a false-hearted lover
Will send you to your grave.

4 They'll hug you and kiss you
And tell you more lies
Than the cross-ties on the railroad,
Or the stars in the skies.

ACTIVITY

Get everyone into a circle.
Pick one person to be the elephant and ask them to stand in the middle.
While singing, the elephant in the middle skips around having fun.
Those on the outside can mime appropriate actions to match the song.

On the line "That he called for another elephant to come,"
everyone wiggles their body and the elephant in
the middle points at someone to come and join him/her.
Keep going until everyone is an elephant!

ONE ELEPHANT

Traditional

THE SUPER SONGBOOK FOR KIDS

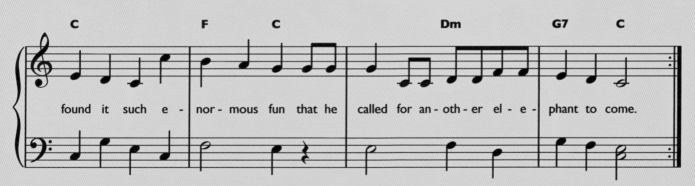

2

Two* elephants went out to play
Upon a spider's web one day.
They found it such enormous fun
That they called for another elephant to come.

change number accordingly

ORANGES AND LEMONS

Steadily

Traditional

"Or - ang - es and lem - ons" say the bells of St.

ONE FINGER, ONE THUMB, KEEP MOVING

Traditional

Fairly fast

mf 1. One fin - ger, one thumb, keep mov - ing, one

fin - ger, one thumb, keep mov - ing, one fin - ger, one thumb, keep

*Repeat as needed in verses 2 to 6

mov - ing, we'll all be mer - ry and bright. _____

2 One finger, one thumb, one arm, keep moving, *etc.*

3 One finger, one thumb, one arm, one leg, keep moving, *etc.*

4 One finger, one thumb, one arm, one leg,
One nod of the head, keep moving, *etc.*

5 One finger, one thumb, one arm, one leg,
One nod of the head, stand up, sit down, keep moving, *etc.*

6 One finger, one thumb, one arm, one leg,
One nod of the head, stand up, sit down,
Turn around, keep moving, *etc.*

KNICKY KNACKY KNOCKY NOO

Traditional

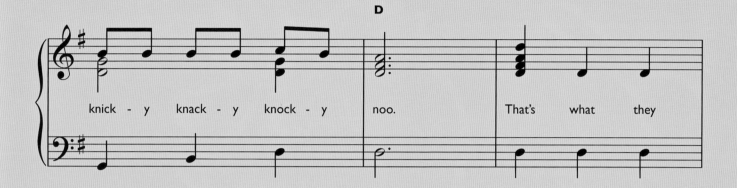

knick - y   knack - y   knock - y   noo.   That's   what   they

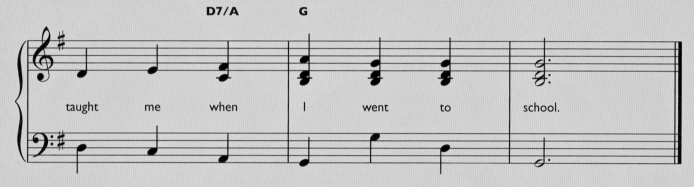

taught   me   when   I   went   to   school.

2
With my hands on my eyes,
What have I here?
These are my eye peepers my teacher dear.
Main thinker, eye peepers, knicky knacky knocky noo.
That's what they taught me when I went to school.

3
With my hands on my nose,
What have I here?
This is my smell boxer my teacher dear.
Main thinker, eye peepers, smell boxer,
Knicky knacky knocky noo.
That's what they taught me when I went to school.

4
With my hands on my mouth,
What have I here?
This is my chatterboxer, *etc.*

5
With my hands on my chin,
What have I here?
This is my chin wagger, *etc.*

6
With my hands on my chest,
What have I here?
This is my air blower, *etc.*

7
With my hands on my stomach,
What have I here?
This is my bread basket, *etc.*

8
With my hands on my lap,
What have I here?
This is my lap sitter, *etc.*

9
With my hands on my knees,
What have I here?
These are my knee knockers, *etc.*

10
With my hands on my foot,
What have I here?
These are my toe tappers, *etc.*

PAT-A-CAKE

Traditional

Moderately

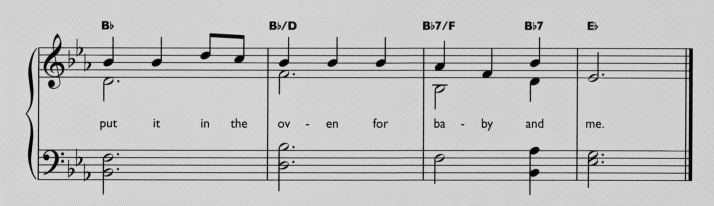

THE GRAND OLD DUKE OF YORK

Traditional

Brightly

G

Oh, the grand old Duke of York, he

POP GOES THE WEASEL

Traditional

Half a pound of two-pen-ny rice,

half a pound of trea-cle, that's the way the

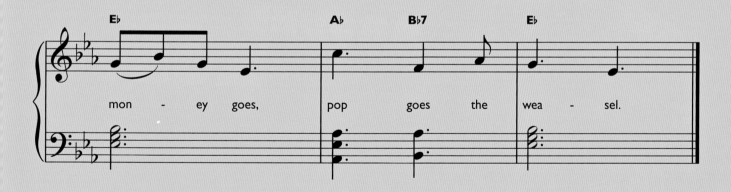

mon-ey goes, pop goes the wea-sel.

Traditional

RING AROUND THE ROSY

Moderately

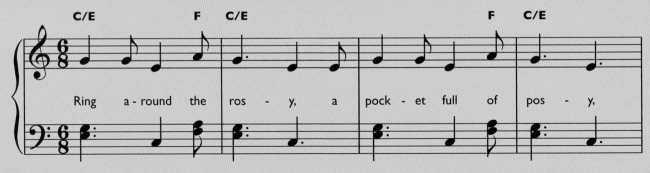

Ring a-round the ros - y, a pock - et full of pos - y,

THE SUPER SONGBOOK FOR KIDS

MARY HAD A LITTLE LAMB

Traditional

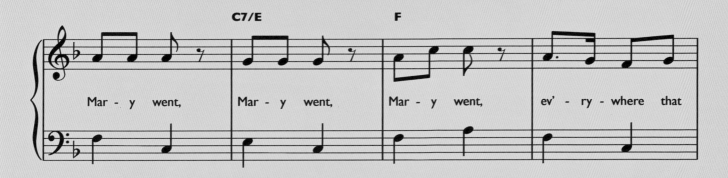

Mar - y went, Mar - y went, Mar - y went, ev' - ry - where that

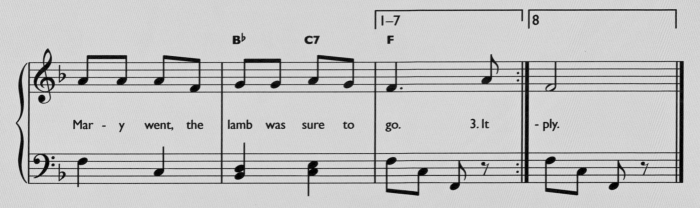

Mar - y went, the lamb was sure to go. 3. It - ply.

2 It followed her to school one day,
School one day, school one day,
It followed her to school one day,
Which was against the rules.

3 It made the children laugh and play,
Laugh and play, laugh and play,
It made the children laugh and play
To see a lamb at school.

4 And so the teacher turned it out,
Turned it out, turned it out,
And so the teacher turned it out,
But still it lingered near.

5 And waited patiently about,
'ly about, 'ly about,
And waited patiently about
Till Mary did appear.

6 "Why does the lamb love Mary so?"
Mary so? Mary so?
"Why does the lamb love Mary so?"
The eager children cry.

7 "Why, Mary loves the lamb, you know."
Lamb, you know, lamb, you know,
"Why, Mary loves the lamb, you know."
The teacher did reply.

TEN GREEN BOTTLES

Traditional

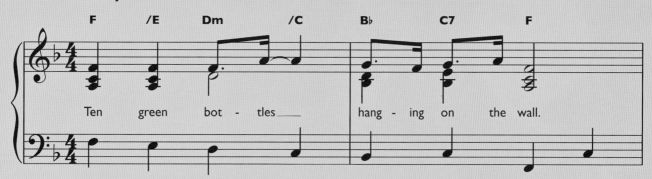

Ten green bot - tles___ hang - ing on the wall.

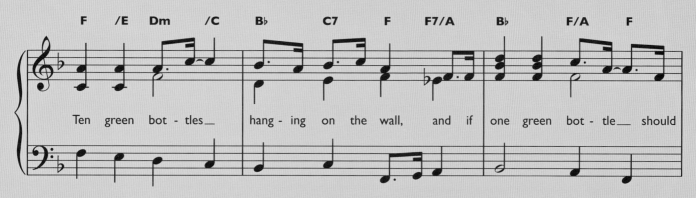

Ten green bot - tles___ hang - ing on the wall, and if one green bot - tle___ should

ac - ci - den - t'ly fall there'll be nine green bot - tles___ hang - ing on the wall.

2 Nine green bottles hanging on the wall.
Nine green bottles hanging on the wall,
And if one green bottle should accidentally fall
There'll be eight green bottles hanging on the wall.

3 Eight green bottles hanging on the wall, *etc.*

4 Seven green bottles hanging on the wall, *etc.*

5 Six green bottles hanging on the wall, *etc.*

6 Five green bottles hanging on the wall, *etc.*

7 Four green bottles hanging on the wall, *etc.*

8 Three green bottles hanging on the wall, *etc.*

9 Two green bottles hanging on the wall, *etc.*

10 One green bottle hanging on the wall.
One green bottle hanging on the wall,
And if that green bottle should accidentally fall
There'll be no green bottles hanging on the wall.

BAA BAA BLACK SHEEP

Traditional

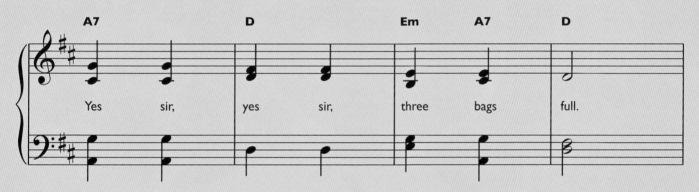

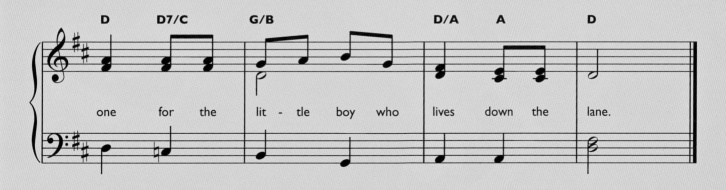

THE SUPER SONGBOOK FOR KIDS

THE MUFFIN MAN

Traditional

Do you know the Muf-fin Man, the Muf-fin Man, the Muf-fin Man? Oh,

do you know the man who sells his muf-fins on the street?

Do you know the Muf-fin Man, the Muf-fin Man, the Muf-fin Man? Oh,

do you know the Muf-fin Man, his wares are such a treat.

YANKEE DOODLE

Traditional

2

Father and I went down to camp
Along with Captain Gooding.
And there we saw the men and boys
As thick as hasty pudding.

Chorus

3

There was Captain Washington
Upon a slapping stallion,
A-giving orders to his men
I guess there was a million.

Chorus

Chorus
Yankee Doodle, keep it up!
Yankee Doodle dandy.
Mind the music and the step
And with the girls be handy.

71

THIS OLD MAN

Traditional

Moderately

2 This old man, he played two,
He played knick-knack on my shoe, *etc.*

3 This old man, he played three…knee, *etc.*

4 This old man, he played four…door, *etc.*

5 This old man, he played five…hive, *etc.*

6 This old man, he played six…sticks, *etc.*

7 This old man, he played seven…up in heaven, *etc.*

8 This old man, he played eight…gate, *etc.*

9 This old man, he played nine…spine, *etc.*

10 This old man, he played ten…once again, *etc.*

Traditional

WHO STOLE THE COOKIE FROM THE COOKIE JAR?

Bright Swing

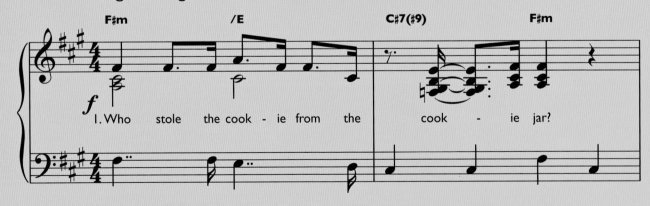

F#m　　　　　/E　　　　　C#7(#9)　　　　F#m

f

1. Who stole the cook - ie from the　　cook - ie jar?

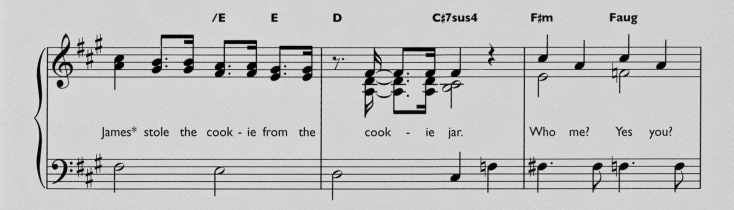

James* stole the cook - ie from the cook - ie jar. Who me? Yes you?

Could - n't be! Could - n't be! Then who stole the cook - ie from the cook - ie jar?

1

Group in unison: Who stole the cookie from the cookie jar?

One person begins by selecting another person. In this example, James.

Starter: JAMES stole the cookie from the cookie jar.

James: Who me?

Group: Yes you!

James: Couldn't be!

Group: Then WHO stole the cookie from the cookie jar?

2

Group: Who stole the cookie from the cookie jar?

James selects another person.

James: SARAH stole the cookie from the cookie jar.

Sarah: Who me?

Group: Yes you!

Sarah: Couldn't be!

Group: Then WHO stole the cookie from the cookie jar?

3

Group: Who stole the cookie from the cookie jar?

Sarah selects another person, etc.

TWO LITTLE DICKIE BIRDS

Traditional

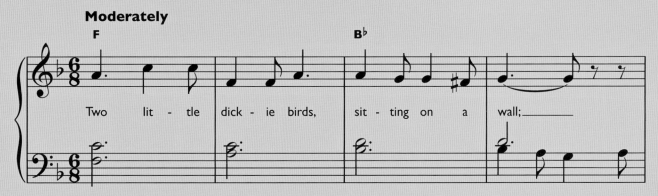

Two lit - tle dick - ie birds, sit - ting on a wall;

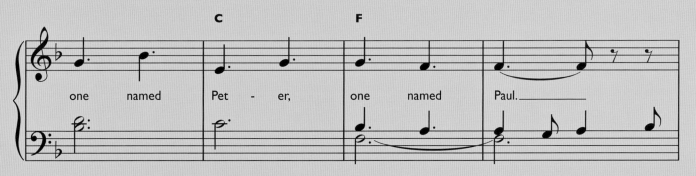

one named Pet - er, one named Paul.

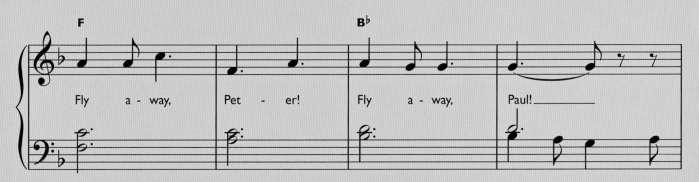

Fly a - way, Pet - er! Fly a - way, Paul!

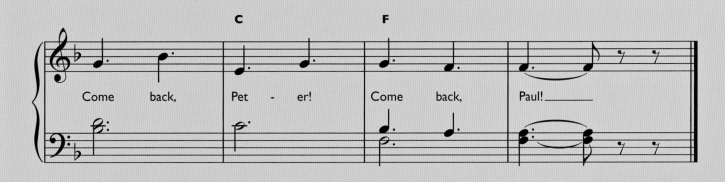

Come back, Pet - er! Come back, Paul!

YOU'LL NEVER GET TO HEAVEN

Moderately

Traditional

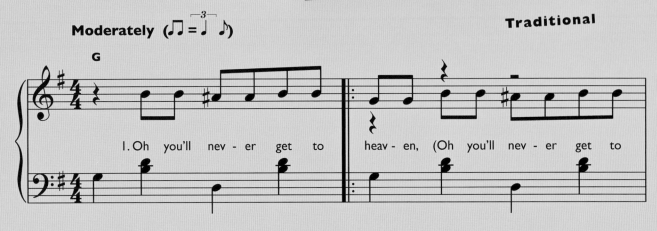

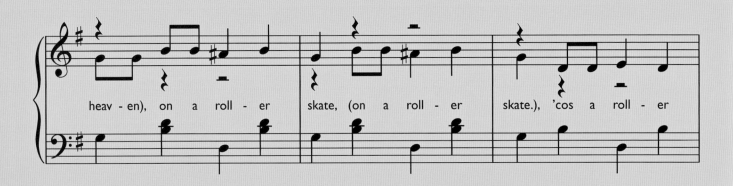

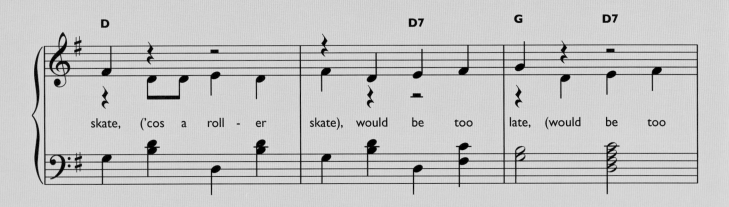

THE SUPER SONGBOOK FOR KIDS

grieve my Lord. I ain't a-gon-na grieve

my Lord no more! 2. Oh you'll nev-er get to

2

Oh you'll never get to heaven
(Oh you'll never get to heaven),
In a rocket ship (in a rocket ship).
'Cos a rocket ship ('cos a rocket ship)
Won't make the trip (won't make the trip).
I ain't a-gonna grieve my Lord no more.

Chorus

3

Oh you'll never get to heaven
(Oh you'll never get to heaven)
On an old tram car (on an old tram car).
'Cos an old tram car ('cos an old tram car)
Won't get that far (won't get that far).
I ain't a-gonna grieve my Lord no more.

Chorus

4

Oh you'll never get to heaven
(Oh you'll never get to heaven)
In a limousine (in a limousine).
'Cos the Lord don't sell ('cos the Lord don't sell)
No gasoline (no gasoline).
I ain't a-gonna grieve my Lord no more.

Chorus

5

Oh you'll never get to heaven
(Oh you'll never get to heaven)
With Superman (with Superman).
'Cos the Lord he is ('cos the Lord he is)
A Batman fan (a Batman fan).
I ain't a-gonna grieve my Lord no more.

Chorus

Chorus

I ain't a-gonna grieve my Lord.
I ain't a-gonna grieve my Lord.
I ain't a-gonna grieve my Lord no more, no more.
I ain't a-gonna grieve my Lord.
I ain't a-gonna grieve my Lord.
I ain't a-gonna grieve my Lord no more.